Ginger Tea Makes Friends

James Barber

RAINCOAST BOOKS

Vancouver

Raincoast Books
8680 Cambie Street
Vancouver, B.C.
V6P 6M9
(604) 323-7100

www.raincoast.com

This book was originally published in 1971 by McClelland and Stewart Ltd.

1 2 3 4 5 6 7 8 9 10

Canadian Cataloguing in Publication Data:

Barber, James, 1923–
Ginger Tea Makes Friends

Includes index.
ISBN 1-55192-284-3

1. Cookery. I. Title.

TX715.B37 2000   641.5   C00-910014-8

Raincoast Books gratefully acknowledges the support of the Government of Canada, through the Book Publishing Industry Development Program, the Canada Council for the Arts and the Department of Canadian Heritage. We also acknowledge the assistance of the Province of British Columbia, through the British Columbia Arts Council.

Printed and bound in Canada.

For Helen – The Enthusiast

Table of Contents

Preface to the New Edition

Way back when, before Martha Stewart, before e-mail, before gourmet websites, when hair was long and money was short, it was the summer of love, a time when everybody wanted to run away and lots of people didn't because they couldn't cook. The Beatles had taught us all how simple music could be, just three chords, so I wrote these books – quick, simple and easy food that made cooking almost as much fun as making love and certainly as easy as strumming a guitar.

The books sold and sold, not just for backpacks but for boats, cottages and bachelor apartments. They never turned up at garage sales; people hung on to them, and I still get regular mail – "Do you still have a spare copy?" – from people who want to give them to their kids but won't part with their own. (An antique book dealer in Victoria recently sold a mint first edition of *Ginger Tea Makes Friends* for $350....) So we reprinted. Even today, all you need to be a good cook is a frypan and these little books.

James Barber

Introduction

Cooking is the simplest way of saying, "I love you." This may sound pretentious as hell, but if you accept it as an essential belief, your cooking will improve – and so will your love life.

There is mystique in the kitchen, mixed in with social acceptance and fancy linen and the right kind of spoons. I learned how to cook in tin mess kits in France, and now I cook on a sailboat at sea or on a beat-up fifty-year-old stove in a kitchen with a table covered in books and a typewriter. I have lots of pots and pans, but mostly I use a heavy iron fry pan with a lid.

I like candles, and I have many saucers to hold them. I use lots of herbs, and I usually measure them in the palm of my hand. A tight squeezed palm is a teaspoon, a medium squeeze is a dessertspoon, and a really open palm is a tablespoon. Measure out some spoonfuls, see how they look in your hand, then forget about spoons and start feeling your food as you cook it.

And that's really the secret to good food: Touch it a bit.

A Simple Soup

1 This is a fall soup, a special for someone you specially want to please. Tomatoes are cheap in the fall, and it is not really a very expensive soup, but is almost obscenely luxurious, a smooth, soft, gentle, fattening, rich thing which makes a very pleasant light supper, particularly by the fire and with, if you can find it, a bottle of that Portuguese green wine very cold.

The important thing is not to boil it, or it will curdle. Gentle it all the way through, gentle in the butter in slivers, stirring all the time, and gentle in the cream, stirring all the time. It should be a pleasant, soft sensation, and once you have started adding things, keep the heat soft and gentle. If you let it boil it will curdle, so be nice to it.

Croutons are just cubes of oldish bread, warmed, rather than fried, very slowly in lots of butter. I usually do them in them in the oven in my big iron frying pan. Melt the butter, toss the cubes in it until they are coated, add a chopped clove of garlic if you wish, or a couple of handfuls of chopped parsley, and put them in a low oven (250 degrees) for an hour or so. Let them cool, and keep in a screw-top jar and use in soups and salads, or just eat them with a glass of wine while you wait for dinner to cook.

And don't forget the dill. If you haven't got any, get some, and start using it on all sorts of things. Cook beets in it, sprinkle it on fish, especially shellfish, and even if you have to finish up one day with a can of soup, throw in a little dill and surprise yourself. Canned tomato soup with dill in it tastes almost as good as the advertisements say it does.

And get a sieve. For many of these recipes the only things you will need are a saucepan and an iron frying pan. But a sieve is useful. And a wooden spoon makes you feel good.

Rainy Day Chicken Livers

2 This is a rainy day dish that I always cook for two – and finish up eating with four.

It needs a bottle of wine – something pretty earthy such as a Gamza, or Bardolino – and a loaf of fresh bread, real bread, and the kind that doesn't come wrapped in plastic.

Also it is cheap, and quick.

Put the potatoes on to boil. Start them in cold water, with salt and mint.

Chop the onion. Cut up the other vegetables into something like one-inch pieces. Slice the mushrooms. Sit back for fifteen minutes.

I always start my cooking with the longest thing and count time from there. Potatoes take about half an hour, and the livers take about ten minutes. So, ten minutes before the potatoes are done, start the onions.

But, before you start, you have about fifteen minutes to sit back and drink some of the vermouth. Or the sherry.

Or the wine. I use vermouth because I like it, but friends use brandy or sherry. Anything with a wine flavour will do.

The important word is gentle. Turn things over. Don't keep dabbing at them with the fork. Just turn them over.

I use chopsticks for a lot of things; it makes for good habits. The Chinese stores sell cooking chopsticks that are joined together at the top by a small string and can hang by the stove.

Use lots of basil. If it comes out of a supermarket jar, crush it before you use it. If you haven't got a mortar and pestle, then use two spoons or, nicer still, put it in the palm of your hand and rub it around with your thumb until it smells nice. And use lots. About twice as much as you think you should. About a spoonful before you crush it. And another pinch for luck. And about half a teaspoon of salt.

Use these things, until they feel right. If you have to cook with measuring spoons and a balance, you might just as well become a druggist, which you won't like. Coat everything with oil, gently. And, when the vegetables begin to change colour and look shiny, add the vermouth or the sherry.

Cook for about six minutes, then add the cream. Bring the heat back up, but don't boil it. Serve it on rice, or potatoes, with peas. Mop up the sauce that's left with bread, finish the wine, sit back and burp.

P-seudo P-sourdough P-sancakes

3 These pancakes are a Saturday or Sunday indulgence, when you have time enough for one of you to stay in bed, while the other sits and reads the paper. There is nothing to the cooking of the pancakes; you just cook one side till there are bubbles on the top, turn it over and cook the other side and eat them with hot maple syrup and butter. They will keep warm wrapped in a cloth in a low oven until you get enough, or if you happen to have your bed in the kitchen you can just eat them as they come. There are people who spend Saturday night on an air mattress on the kitchen floor just to be there in the morning, but that is close to addiction, which, until a local chapter of Pancakes Anonymous is formed, should be avoided.

But there are other aspects of these pancakes, which should be noted. The first one up makes tea, peels an orange, gets the morning paper down off the roof, and delivers these three things, preferably with a flower and a candle, to the bedside. He then puts on the coffee while he makes the pancake mixture, feeds the cat, avoids last night's dishes, and (this is a secret) sprinkles dry coffee on the stove burner so that the whole apartment begins to smell like coffee should taste.

By the time the coffee is ready the pancakes will be ready to cook. You know how to do this. Now, the first one you will have to try. Just to see if it is good enough for your mate. It will be. And perhaps that, you will think, was an accident, and you should try the next one. So you mix another batch, and finally deliver them, smiling, together with the maple syrup (if you can find Swedish lingonberries in a delicatessen then so much the better than anything else in the world), and butter, and hot coffee, and of course yourself, a portable radio and a couple of spare cushions.

The greatest pleasure comes in not answering the phone or doorbell.

Corned Beef Hash

4 Twenty-five years ago, I learned to cook corned beef hash in a mess kit over an open fire, in a field under an apple tree. With a girl. The army gave us the corned beef, we stole the onions and potatoes from a farm, and she brought some bacon fat to cook with.

Nowadays I am a little more sophisticated about it but the flavour is still there – the crisp, almost-burned outside and the squishy, steaming inside. Kids like it and they particularly like their fathers to make it. Wives like it, people on boats like it, it's great on beaches and just as good in the kitchen on a Sunday afternoon.

And it's easy. And cheap.

I used canned corned beef. Slice the onions thinly and chop them into half-inch strips. Slice the corned beef and put it in a bowl with the onions, a little more pepper than you think you should use, and a level teaspoonful of salt. Get your fingers in it; squish it about until its well mixed, then throw in an egg.

Squish it some more with the potatoes. Some people use a fork at this stage, but fingers are better.

Put a little oil, or bacon fat, or butter, in the frying pan (preferably a heavy one), heat it just to smoking, and spread the mixture about half an inch thick – or three-quarters, depending on how much you like the crispy outside.

Sprinkle the top with mustard powder, about a teaspoonful or a bit more, and spread it with a knife or your fingers. Cook it on a medium fire until it slides readily in the pan, when the bottom will have a well-baked crust. About ten minutes.

Now comes the trick. Put a large plate over the pan, hold it steady, and turn the whole thing over. The crisp side is now topside on the plate. Put the pan back on the fire, add a little more fat, and slide the whole thing gently but quickly back and forth for another ten minutes.

Sprinkle and pat more mustard onto the top (the crispy side), while it's cooking, and when its done slide the whole thing out onto a plate.

Good with cabbage. Slice the cabbage thinly, cut out the core, and place in a heavy saucepan with a couple of table-spoons of oil, a tablespoonful of water, half a teaspoonful of salt, and a good sprinkling of pepper. Don't be scared of the pepper. Put the lid on, cook over medium heat, shaking frequently – about ten minutes, until it's just cooked, just transparent.

CORNED BEEF HASH

Add together

sliced corned beef

one onion

or

two

chopped fine...

3 medium sized

potatoes grated coarsely

in a bowl

squish together

then one egg

fork stir to mix

Fix Mix into cake ½" to ¾" thick in

Sprinkle with 1½ tsps mustard

cook medium heat for 10 min.

to turn over cover frying pan with plate

flip

and slide back to cook other side. Add ½ tsp of hot mustard...

THE HASH WILL HAVE A THICK BROWN CRUST ON BOTH SIDES EAT WITH CABBAGE

Omelette

5 Put anything in this omelette, like grated cheese, or honey, or mushrooms sliced and gently fried in butter with basil, or shrimps or crabs with dill, or caviar (the cheap kind is enough and it's a fantastic Sunday breakfast) or tomatoes and onions sliced and fried with a little olive oil and some oregano or crumbled bacon or parsley or some just fried bean sprouts with a little onion and a crushed flower of star anise.

And if you want to make a lunch of it, most elegant, make borscht first, preferably the day before. Get two bunches of fresh beets, cut off tops and bottoms, slice them, put in about a quart and a half of water, a teaspoonful of dill, a pinch of salt and a teaspoonful of sugar.

Boil them all for an hour. Strain, put the beets in vinegar to eat later with cheese, and put the soup (it's purple and looks like good wine) in the refrigerator. Serve cold, with lots of sour cream and chopped cucumber (skin on). Very good with Portuguese Vinho Verde.

Do it with style, and let it take five minutes. Borscht in the bowls, sour cream ready, cucumber chopped. Then quick, the eggs, six for two of you, and a soup ladle holds exactly three when you come to put them in the pan.

Heat the pan (keep the flame high) until water flicked on it bounces. Dump in the butter and swish it around until it foams (but don't let it get brown). Quick with the eggs, and immediately stir with the fork flat on the bottom of the pan. Vigorously. Until the eggs are just set. Then you have a minute.

Leave the pan to sit, put in the filling, fold over one-third of the omelette in the pan, and then turn it all on to a plate. Another minute for the next one and you're away. I once cooked forty-four omelettes for a party, one after the other, in an hour, with a collection of different fillings. It's a great trick to learn.

A heavy pan is best. Mine is a Norwegian one, about eight dollars. Don't use it for anything else, and never wash it. If anything sticks, scour it with salt. The more you use it, the better it gets. Lots of butter.

Coq au Vin

6 When the autumn leaves start to fall chickens are cheap. Not the little, skinny mini-skirted spring chickens, but the tough old heavies who just can't make it any more in the egg parlours. They call them Grade B, and the sell for about forty cents a pound.

While you are shopping, pick up half a pound of small onions. Really small ones, little round pretty ones. And about a quarter pound of meaty back bacon. If you're short of money get bacon ends and cut off the fat. And a bottle of half-decent burgundy. The better the wine, the better the dish. Don't, unless you are a confirmed masochist, use Canadian wine for cooking. And get a bunch of parsley. Keep what you don't use in a plastic bag in the refrigerator. A loaf of French bread is also timely.

Now, accept the fact that it's easy. Place two or three ounces of butter in the heavy iron frying pan, and brown the chicken (which of course you have defrosted) all over. Put it aside in a warm place – the oven if you want, very low, and brown the onions (whole) and the bacon (in strips) in the same pan. While the onions are browning, joint the chicken – wings, legs, and the carcass – into four pieces. Put it all together in the pan, turn the heat up high and add half the wine. Have a glass for yourself while you are at it. Crush a clove of garlic, put that in, and a little salt. The rest of the salt goes in when you are ready to serve. A little pepper, and a bouquet garni. Put the lid on, turn down the heat to very slow, and leave it for about a few hours. Take a book and another glass of wine to the bath, with a note on the door, if you are a mother, to say that you are cooking dinner and must not be disturbed.

In three hours or so (time is not important) it will be ready. Take out the bouquet garni, thicken the pot a little with *beurre manié*, and add a little salt to taste and brown the sliced bread in butter or cooking oil (not olive oil this time). Put the chicken on the table, liberally sprinkled with chopped parsley.

Serve it with the bread, and green peas, and rice, or mashed potatoes. That's it – Coq au Vin, a French name for a simple dish.

A bouquet garni is a bunch of parsley stalks (keep the leaves for the final serving). Tie the stalks in a bunch with a bay leaf, and a sprig of thyme, and leave a long end on the string so that you can find it later. If you can't find fresh herbs, use Spice Islands bottled bouquet garni tied up in muslin, and if you can't be bothered with the muslin, just dump it in the pot. It tastes the same, but looks better with the little extra care.

Beurre manié is a mixture of butter and flour. About twice as much butter as flour. Mix it together into a paste and roll it into little balls, about a quarter of an inch across. To thicken, add the balls one or two at a time to the pan until it is thick enough. Shake; not stir, because the stirring will break up the meat. Bring to the boil, and that's it. *Bon Appétit.*

COQ au VIN

AN **OLD** CHICKEN

"CHEAP CHEAP"

brown it in butter s-l-o-w-l-y

AND PUT IN A WARM PLACE

BROWN

ONIONS AND BACON

JOINT THE **CHIC KEN**

ADD 1/2 THE WINE AND A BOUQUET GARNI.

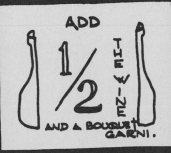

AND THE ONIONS ETC A CLOVE GARLIC A LITTLE SALT TO THE POT

SLOW FIRE VERY SLOW

WHILE YOU TAKE A BATH

REMOVE THE HERBS THICKEN A LITTLE WITH .BEURRE MANIE. SALT TO TASTE. SPRINKLE WITH FRESH CHOPPED PARSLEY

AND SERVE

"MAGNIFIQUE"

WITH A FRENCH ACCENT, THE REST OF THE WINE AND FRIED CROUTONS. NOBODY WILL KNOW IT IS JUST CHICKEN STEW.

Hurry Up Clam Chowder

Fish Needs Fennel. Remember that. The most ancient, sad and dejected piece of fish in the world can be transformed by fennel seeds into something exciting.

The little hard kernels need grinding up. If you haven't got a mortar, use two spoons. Put the fennel in one and the other on top and press hard with your thumb while you wriggle them about.

Dill is almost as good, but a better herb for shellfish. The fennel has a more exciting taste, which comes through the smoothness of the potatoes and clam juice.

This is not a prescription recipe. Onions are essential, and so is some sort of bacon, even if it is only bacon fat left over from the breakfast frying pan. Celery is nice, but so is green pepper, and so are thin sliced mushrooms, or even leeks. It is capable of almost infinite extension by the use of soup cubes. I usually feed two people with this amount. But if two or four more arrive there is always another potato, and another soup cube, and another cup of water. And another stick of celery and…

There is nothing quite like a wet afternoon digging clams and coming home to a hot bath and clam chowder. Kids like it; fathers become enormously popular. After a movie or a walk it is a genuine half-hour recipe which is much more fun than waiting for the pizza delivery man to arrive with a bill for thirteen or fourteen dollars and what you save on pizza you can spend on beer or a bottle of wine.

If you can't dig clams, then the canned minced ones are the cheapest and best alternative. Everything except the fennel is usually available in the corner store, and if you want to plan ahead for a lot of people then get all the nice things you like for the chowder, and make garlic bread and put a dish of chopped parsley on the side and some one-inch lengths of green onion for people to dump in as they like.

Leeks in half-inch slices are very good in chowder if you want to make it a family meal. Fry them a little first in butter or oil or bacon fat. Don't worry about making too much – somehow it always disappears.

HURRY UP CLAM CHOWDER

CHOP 3 SLICES BACON
2 STICKS CELERY
1 MEDIUM ONION
INTO
HALF INCH BITS

FRY BACON TRANSPARENT IN ITS OWN FAT

THEN...

ONION AND CELERY TRANS-PARENT TOO.

NOW

CAN CLAMS

JUST THE JUICE. AND A BAYLEAF HALF A LEMON DASH PEPPER HALF TSPN DILL OR FENNEL AND

HALF TSPN CURRY PWDR

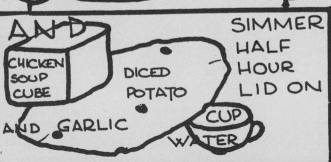

SIMMER HALF HOUR LID ON

ADD CLAMS FOR FIVE MINUTES

Lamb Chops Sofia

Sofia was tall and elegant and beautiful, and she thought that lamb chops were a last resort.

Lamb Chops Sofia evolved itself while she lighted the fire and washed my last week's dishes and swept the floor and made my bed and fed the cat and emptied the bath and generally behaved like a liberated woman. It is easy to make, with a nice long time to sit and decide that the day wasn't so bad after all. There is also only one pot to clean, and if you put in enough vegetables it is what the dieticians call a balanced meal.

I buy cheap lamb chops, shoulder chops. Any lamb at all can be made nice with a little love and care, and all lamb improves at least one hundred percent if you can possibly arrange to leave it marinating in the refrigerator overnight. Even if you live in one room and haven't got a refrigerator, meat will keep in a marinade for twenty-four hours.

Marinades are a personal thing. Try about half and half oil and vinegar (or wine), a bit of fine chopped onion, a little salt, a little pepper, and (for lamb) some basil or rosemary or oregano. Lemon juice is nice too. Don't be scared of oregano – use lots. You don't need to make enough marinade to cover the meat, just mix a bit in a plate, dip both sides, and turn it occasionally. And if you have a cat put it somewhere inaccessible. I once had a cat which ate six marinating lamb chops in ten minutes, while I took a shower.

Fry the chops quickly till they are brown, then turn down the heat. The rest is easy. Take a look occasionally, and if it is getting too dry, dump in a spoonful or two of water. Or wine. If you want to pretty it up, sprinkle a little chopped parsley before you serve, and put one lamb chop on each plate, on top of the rice.

Le Big Secret

9 Just think of them as pancakes and it's easy. Not hotcakes, but just some rather special pancakes that you are going to make for a weekend breakfast or lunch. Then, if you want to show off one day with a great flaming flourish at the end of dinner, you will know how. Your guest will be impressed, and you may well have learned a new social grace – such as what to say to the boss the morning after you have set his wife's wig on fire.

Crepes or pancakes, the mix is the same:

    7 ounces flour
    3 eggs
    1 teaspoon sugar
    1/4 pint milk
    A good pinch of salt
    2 tablespoons melted butter
    1 ounce cognac or rum

The rum is essential for crepes; optional for pancakes. In either case, nice.

Mix the flour, sugar and salt in one bowl. Beat together the eggs, milk, butter and cognac in another bowl – and slowly mix them into the dry ingredients. Keep beating until everything is smooth. Don't bother with a beater. Use a fork. Now leave it at least two hours or overnight in the refrigerator. Just ignore it. That's all the making there is. The rest is cooking.

For pancakes, check that the mixture is thin. If it is any thicker than cream, add water and mix in with a fork until it's thin enough.

Heat your cast iron pan on a medium heat. Melt about half a teaspoon of butter all over the pan, and pour in enough batter to cover the bottom thinly. Swirl it about a bit so it covers. The mix should be thin enough to run.

Cook about a minute, and turn it over with a spatula or (all this needs is courage and nobody looking) toss it. Another minute and it will be done.

Sprinkle sugar all over, squeeze about a quarter of a lemon on the sugar, roll it up in the pan and roll it on to a plate. A little more sugar, a little more lemon juice, and you have the traditional English pancake.

Crepes you cook the same way in a little pan. And you stack them up until you have about three per person. It's best to do it in the afternoon if you insist on showing off at dinner.

You can fill them with smoked salmon or crab, and cook them in a hollandaise sauce, or you can be really vulgar and ostentatious and do the whole Crepes Suzette trip. Whatever you do will be expensive.

For Crepes Suzette, cream a quarter-pound butter with three good tablespoonfuls sugar (icing sugar is best), a tablespoon of grated lemon rind, and the rind and juice of an orange. And about an ounce of Cointreau (or Grand Marnier or Curaçao).

Really cream the butter and sugar. Then add the other things slowly, and keep mixing. If it separates, don't worry too much. The heat will fix things for you.

Heat the big heavy pan, dump in the butter mixture, and cook it until it bubbles. Then dip each little crepe from the pre-cooked stack into the mixture, turn it over, fold it into quarters, and push it to one side of the pan.

When they are all done, spread them back over the pan, sprinkle them with sugar, and pour about an ounce of brandy and Cointreau (or whatever) over them. Stand back; light a match and whoosh. Easy.

SSSSSSSH

LE BIG SECRET

CREPES ARE SO

EASY EASY EASY
HO HUM NOTHING TO IT
EASY EASY EASY
ANYBODY CAN DO IT
EASY EASY EASY
AMAZE YOUR FRIENDS
SIX EASY LESSONS
OH MY DEAR, NOTHING
TO IT. HELEN IS SO
CLEVER. EASY EASY EASY

THEY JUST PANCAKES

WITH STUFF ON THEM

7 OZ. FLOUR
1 TSP. SUGAR
PINCH SALT
1

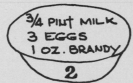

3/4 PINT MILK
3 EGGS
1 OZ. BRANDY
2

TWO BOWLS

BEAT BOWL 2

EGGS WITH
2 TABLESPOONS
MELTED BUTTER

AND S-L-O-W-L-Y
MIX INTO FLOUR
ETC (BOWL No 1)

VERY SMOOTH

HOURS OR ALL NIGHT BUT

LEAVE IT ALONE

THIN IT WITH WATER TO A THIN CREAM

LITTLE BUTTER
MEDIUM HEAT.
TO JUST GOLDEN

FRY GENTLY

TURN ONCE.
BIG PAN — PANCAKES
LITTLE PAN — CREPES

PANCAKES:
SPRINKLE LEMON
JUICE AND SUGAR,
ROLL UP.

OR

CREPES: 1/4 lb butter, 2 oz sugar,
2 oz Cointreau, 2 oz. brandy, orange
juice, orange peel and lemon peel
both chopped. Heat to bubbling,
dip crepes both sides, fold to
quarters at side of pan. FLAME.

Spaghetti anda Stuff

Just cook it long enough – and slowly. What you don't eat, put in little plastic bags and place in the freezer of your refrigerator.

It's a tomato sauce, originally for lasagna. If you want to stiffen it up in a hurry, fry half a pound of hamburger until it separates, then pour on the sauce and cook together for half an hour.

If you want it even thicker, add tomato paste. Canned tomatoes are better and cheaper for spaghetti than most fresh ones. If you do use fresh ones, skin them first by putting them in boiling water for a couple of minutes. The skin will peel off easily.

The lemon is important. Take it out before you store the sauce. Use lots of basil, at least a teaspoonful, and half as much oregano.

Now we come to the serious business. There are two tests of true love in the kitchen. One is making Eggs Benedict; the other is fresh pasta, or "pasta fatta in casa." It takes time, so do it on a rainy Saturday. Cook it while the sauce is on the fire.

Spaghetti, lasagna, macaroni and rigatoni, they're all the same stuff – pasta. And there is no taste in the world like lasagna made with fresh pasta. So, Lasagna al forno.

3 eggs, well beaten.
Small teaspoon salt.
1 pound flour.
5 tablespoons water.

Mix it soft to a ball. You might need a little more water. Sprinkle a board with flour and knead the dough for about fifteen minutes with the heel of your hand. Sprinkle a little flour around occasionally so it won't stick.

It's a nice time to talk to people. That's why good bread-makers become such nice people.

Twist the dough off into six parts. One at a time put them on a board and roll them as thinly as you can. I use a wine bottle for a rolling pin. Sprinkle a bit more flour about. It's very elastic, so it's hard work.

Fold it over a couple of times, and do it over again. Three times. For lasagna, cut the final thin dough into two-inch strips, and put them somewhere on a clean cloth to dry for about an hour.

The sauce is beginning to smell good by now and might need half a cup of water.

Now, homemade pasta needs only half as much cooking time as the commercial kind. Lots of boiling salted water, and cook the strips of lasagna three to four minutes. Take them out and drain.

Butter a dish (lots of butter), a layer of cooked lasagna, a layer of crumbled mozzarella cheese, a thin layer of either chopped Italian sausage, or salami, or hamburger rolled into little balls.

Another layer of thinly sliced hardboiled eggs, and sprinkle it all with Parmesan cheese.

Now the thin tomato sauce over all, and start the layers all over again – twice, maybe three times, depending on how thick your pasta is.

Finish top with tomato sauce and a few knobs of butter. Bake at 350° to 375°F for half an hour.

If you use bought pasta, that's okay. But boil it ten minutes.

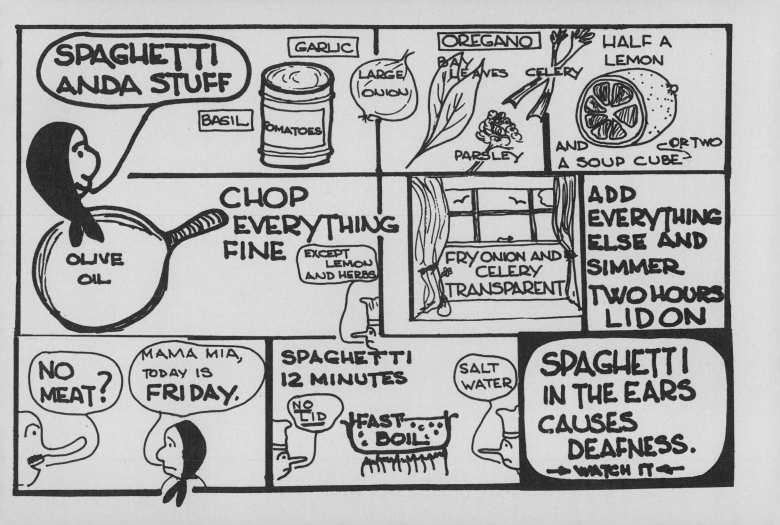

Poor Man Pizza

11 If you live in a basement suite with a fire-breathing landlady who doesn't want you to cook, to come in late, to have visitors after 10:00 p.m., smoke, drink, bathe more than once a week or turn over in bed because it wears out the sheets, then you have a problem.

This recipe is specifically for basement suite dwellers who hide the hotplate and the frying pan under the bed. It can be made by others, by children for supper, and by hungry drunks as a measure of their sobriety, by diesel mechanics wishing to get their fingernails clean and by the totally incompetent who normally manage to mess up the preparation of something so simple as a can of sardines.

It is simple and foolproof. Nothing you can do to the dough can spoil it. It is indigestible, filling and as interesting as you care to make it.

The only care that must be taken is in the frying. The oil must be hot, but not smoking, so that after five minutes cooking the underside is a golden brown, not too hard but just crisp. It is so cheap to make that if you foul it up you just throw it away, feed it to the dog or keep it till next morning as a special treat for the seagulls on the beach.

POOR MAN PIZZA

QUICKER THAN PHONING

DUMP IN A BOWL
1 CUP FLOUR
1 TSP BAKING PWDR
½ TSP. SALT
4, 5 OR 6 TBLSP. WATER

MAUL IT ABOUT

BE ROUGH WITH IT

NOW ← THROW IN A HANDFUL OF GRATED CHEESE AND HALF A TSPN OREGANO.

MAUL IT MORE

ROLL IT OUT WITH A BOTTLE ABOUT ½" THICK

¼" OIL IN FRYING PAN — HOT BUT NOT SMOKING.

IF IT SMOKES TAKE IT OFF TILL IT STOPS

CAREFULLY PUT IN DOUGH. LOW HEAT, 5 MINUTES. TURN OVER.

PUT WHAT YOU LIKE ON TOP. COOK 5 MIN MORE. (SLICED TOMATO, FRIED BACON, ANCHOVIES FRIED SLICED MUSHROOMS, CANNED SHRIMP AND DILL, AVOCADO, SALAMI — ANYTHING). THEN MORE CHEESE.

IT'S NOT PIZZA BUT IT'S NOT BAD

Chinese Food in Five Minutes

Stir-frying is a basic technique of Chinese cooking. It is a quick, easy and energetic method that requires your complete attention for five minutes and is something well worth learning. The food is bright and attractive, better than you get in all but the best Chinese restaurants and as economical or extravagant as you wish to make it.

The first time I suggest that you start with very simple ingredients. Bean sprouts, green pepper, a couple sticks of celery and either green beans or bok choy (that's the Chinese cabbage with thick white stems). Get a little of each. Bean sprouts are in the supermarket in packets or loose in Chinatown. A handful of beans, a quarter pound of mushrooms and a bunch of green onions will do it. Root ginger – not powdered – is the only kind for getting the right taste. Garlic, powdered if you must, but it's much better to learn about it fresh. Just crush a clove with the side of a knife and the skin will shake off. Then chop it fine.

First, put on the rice. One cup rice, two cups water, a pinch of salt, bring to a boil, stir once, put lid on tight and turn the heat down to the lowest you can. No peeking, just leave it for twenty minutes. While it's cooking, cut the vegetables.

Celery, green beans in one-inch lengths. Little mushrooms halved, big ones sliced. Bok choy in one-inch lengths. Green onions in one-inch lengths, but separate the white part from the green. Cut an onion into coarse pieces (about one inch).

If you haven't got a wok (Chinese frying pan and worth getting) then use a heavy frying pan, fairly big. If you haven't got a heavy frying pan, make up your mind to get one. You're going to need it if you like my cooking. Start when the rice has been on for fifteen minutes.

Cut three or four strips of fat bacon into quarter inch slices. Or use bacon ends, which are cheaper. Or hog jowl, which is even cheaper. Fry it with the garlic until transparent. Grate in about a quarter inch of the gingerroot (don't peel it, just grate it on the coarse grater).

The pan will be hot and on the point of smoking. Keep it hot, dump in the celery and turn it over and over (from underneath) in the fat. Thirty seconds later put in the bok choy, beans, the onion and green pepper.

Keep turning it over. Don't mess about from the top, get under it. Coat every thing with the bacon fat and keep it moving. Use a pancake turner or anything else big.

Thirty seconds later put in the bean sprouts. Pepper, a good pinch of salt, keep turning over and over, pan very hot. Now the mushrooms, and the green onions (the white part). Lid on the pan (it will be ready in two minutes).

A teaspoonful of cornstarch dissolved in a little water, a soup cube in half a cup of hot water. Take off the lid one minute before it's ready, put in the soup stock and green parts of the onions. Turn it all. Put in the cornstarch. Turn it all. Cook thirty seconds. Take it off the stove into a dish, eat on rice. Good with beer.

Chinese FOOD IN 5 MINUTES

1 heavyweight or wok

4 strips fat bacon chopped up

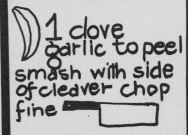

1 clove garlic to peel smash with side of cleaver chop fine

grate about 1/4" fresh ginger root into pan...add garlic

half an onion.. slice coarsely into chunks

then...the and/ors celery beans green pepper bok choy green onions...

mushrooms but not potatoes cut into 1" lengths High Heat..add vegetables.. stir fry

Add 1 packet 1/2 lb bean sprouts

salt pepper

Leave lid on 2 mins. or add soup cube dissolved in 1/2 cup water and 1 tsp. cornstarch in a little water 1 minute each

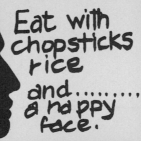

Eat with chopsticks rice and........ a happy face.

Buttered Crab

13 Use canned crab if you have to, but fresh is better. This is a ridiculously simple, completely foolproof recipe which is just made for bachelors, spinsters, apartment hermits and ladies who get picked up on buses and want to take him home.

This is one of the few canned meals that appeals to me. All you need to buy is a bottle of dry sherry, a couple or so of flowers and a candle, and you will have a dinner party of considerable elegance for two.

Just get things ready for the crab, shove it in the fridge and forget it. Let him, her, or whatever your fancy is, pour a glass of sherry and relax. Open a can of consommé (you may hide out in the bathroom and do it if you want to be thought really clever), dilute it with three-quarters of the water recommended, and heat it. While it's heating let the hot tap run on two mugs or cups or whatever you want to serve your consommé in. As soon as the soup is hot, pour it into the mugs and quickly dump in an ounce or two of sherry. And if you want to be elegant, float a thin slice of lemon. That's it. Stage One over.

Now do the crab. Just like the picture. If there is fresh asparagus in the stores, cook it fifteen minutes with a squeeze of lemon over the heads, and serve with melted butter. But if there isn't any fresh, used canned asparagus. Put it in the refrigerator for a bit, open it, drain it and serve it cold with melted butter poured over it. Just like that.

Saturday lunch, midnight supper, after a movie, when your mother-in-law arrives, somebody special, or if you just plain want to make a pig of yourself on crab.

Zabaglione

14   Zabaglione is the only dessert anybody needs to know. It is the best food in the world for two, sensual, easy, rich, mildly intoxicating and so nice that no matter what you have done with the rest of the dinner it will be forgiven and forgotten.

The making is foolproof, if you take care of just two things. It is nice to get the egg whites and yolks separated, but it doesn't matter if you are a bit sloppy. It is nice to use fresh eggs that haven't been in the refrigerator, but it doesn't matter that much. It is nice to use Marsala, but sherry is okay and so is Madeira. I know people who have developed a taste for it with whiskey, but none of these things really matters. What is important is to keep beating it, and not to use boiling water.

I just take a saucepan of boiling water off the stove and use that, topping it up occasionally to keep it hot. If you leave the bottom of the bowl unbeaten while you light cigarettes or display your etchings it will curdle or turn into a custard. Which has no appeal at all.

It has been around a long time as a food and an aphrodisiac. The Romans like it, and the Italians, and the French and the Spaniards. I have had a Greek version of it made with that aromatic Greek honey (this needs a lot of care and a lot of beating), and in Belgium a Dutch bottled version of it is very popular. But best of all it is fresh made, and eaten very quietly, at body temperature.

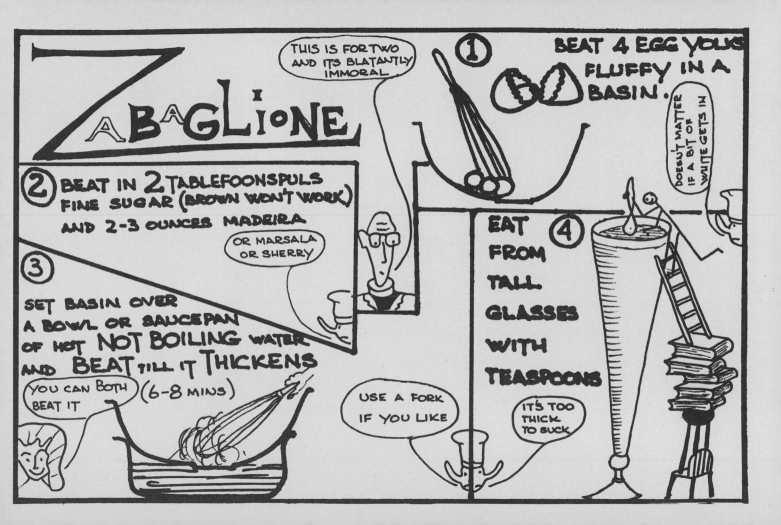

Six Pak Stu

15

This is a nice, thick, belly-lining stew that makes a pound and a half of meat go a long way. I like to make it on a Sunday afternoon, put it in the oven and go for a walk.

With heavy rye bread, and Brussels sprouts or braised leeks, it is a pleasantly satisfying meal with friends and a case of beer.

If you want to be elegant, and call it *Carbonades de Boeuf à la Flamande*, then feel happy about it. Light candles, put flowers on the table, get a good rough Burgundy and cook a lot of asparagus.

The only care you must take is in making the roux. That's the mixing in of the flour, after you have fried the meat. There should be sufficient fat left in the pan to cook the flour and, if you scrape around a lot and make sure that every bit of sediment gets mixed in, it will taste much better when it gets to the table. But cook the roux gently, very low heat, stirring all the time, with the fork held flat on the bottom of the pan.

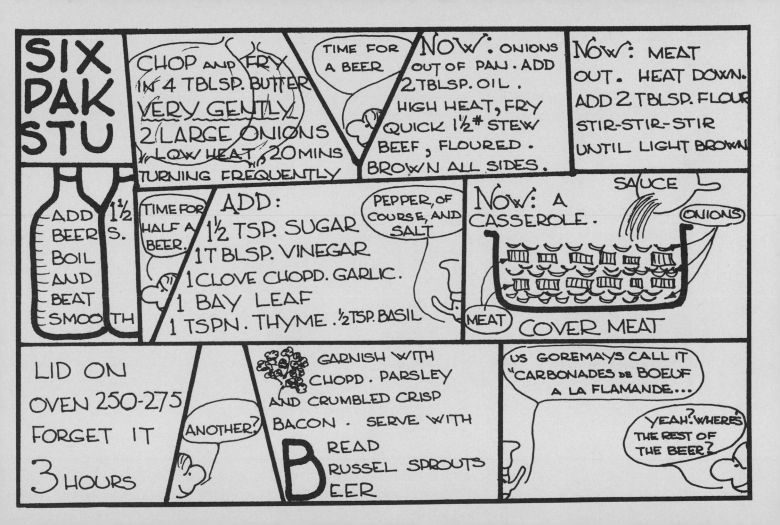

Two's Company Chicken

Gin?

If this recipe used juniper berries, nobody would make it. Because juniper berries are hard to find. The distillers buy a lot of them to make gin.

Gin is not fashionable in kitchens. But, if you learn to cook with it, you will always keep some on hand. It's good for rubbing backs, or cleaning false teeth, for thinning paint or anesthetizing flies. In cooking, it does a lot for almost any drab meat.

Something happens in the cooking and instead of a tame domesticated bland chicken flavour, there comes a most aromatic smell, and the taste of wild game, like partridges that have been feeding all summer on berries.

When you make the stuffing, just put in enough to make it stick together. And the better the bread, the better the stuffing. Rye bread, or sourdough, or good crusty French bread, or even cooked rice.

It's all simple, which is just as well because most beginners with a bottle of gin tend to become a little confused after the second basting.

Try to get root ginger if you can. The flavour is much better than powdered. Most supermarkets sell it and it will keep in the fridge wrapped in a piece of foil until you want to cook some Chinese food.

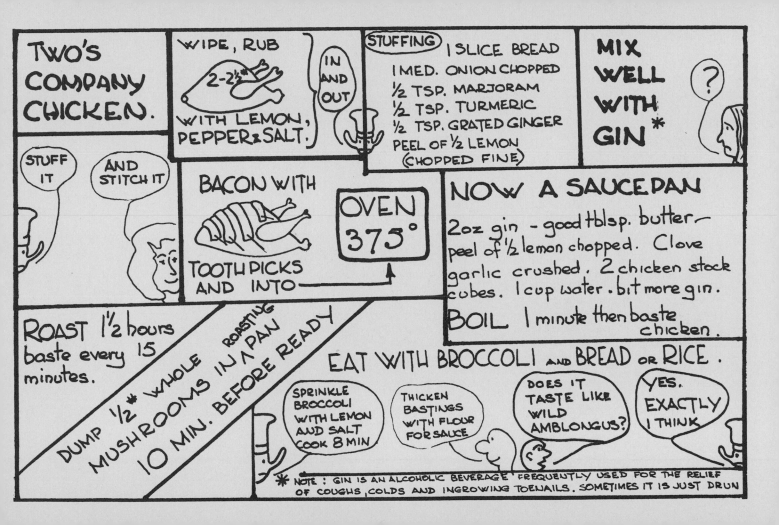

Curry

17

Cardamom seeds are little soft white fibrous shells, which you open with your thumbnail and find inside half a dozen little hard black seeds. They must be crushed, either with a mortar and pestle, or set on a board and rolled with a beer bottle.

Beer is the only drink for a good curry, or, if you are feeling wealthy, gin and tonic. Tea is good too, but this curry is a party dish, a sharing dish, and is extremely economical. Six people can eat off one pound of meat, although there is nothing wrong with more if you feel like it.

I buy cheap imported lamb, which may look fat at the beginning, but don't worry. Two things will happen to the fat if you cook it gently and long enough. First of all, there will be chemical changes which firm it up and make it taste extremely sweet, and any excess will come to the top of the pot during the cooling overnight, and can be lifted off with a spoon.

Apart from cardamom seeds, the big secret in cooking curry is to fry the curry powder. It will go dark brown, and smell bright and fiercely bitter and clean out your sinuses and maybe make your eyes water. Very slow cooking is also essential. The man who showed me this recipe insisted that a curry was not a curry until you had slept with it, and in his restaurant there were indeed cooks curled up by their copper pots, large, two foot copper pots with small charcoal fires underneath.

I sometimes make a curry late at night, and let it simmer till breakfast. The meat may disintegrate, but it doesn't matter, the whole thing becomes a very rich bitter-sweet, hot and delicious thick sauce to eat over rice. And it is infinitely extendable by the pretties you eat with it. Rice on a plate, curry on the rice, and goodies on the curry. None of this elegant dishing up – it is a nice, messy together dish, as complicated or as simple as you wish.

If you are going to fry bananas, don't get them too green. The ripest bananas are best. I usually buy the ones on special that are just beginning to turn black. Peel them, cut them in half then lengthwise, so that each banana is four pieces. Fry them in butter both sides, till they are soft, lift them out of the pan to a dish, and dust them liberally with cinnamon. Highly addictive.

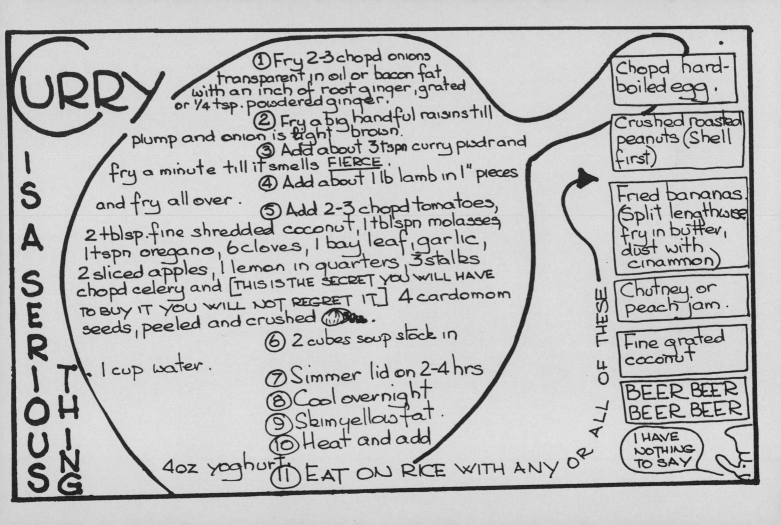

Fried Rice

Fried Rice seems to have become an afterthought in North America. "Sweet and Sour Spare Ribs... Chow Mein... some prawns... and some rice... no make that Fried rice... how long will it be?"

And it shouldn't be. This recipe is very close to a Javanese dish called Nasi Goreng, and it is a meal unto itself, an extremely attractive dish of bright colours and exotic taste that is simple to make and can be as imaginative as your pocket will allow.

Always, when you cook rice, cook too much, and keep what you don't eat covered in the fridge. So the first thing you had better learn to do is cook rice properly. Have nothing to do with instant rice; it has neither taste nor substance. Brown rice has a tendency to get soggy in fried dishes, and I always use long grain white rice for this particular dish, mainly because it looks so pretty.

One cup of rice, two cups of water and a pinch of salt. Put it in the heaviest pot you have, bring it quickly to the boil with the cover off, put the lid on tight and forget it for twenty minutes with the heat as low as you can get it. An asbestos pad under the pot helps keep the heat down. Don't touch it, don't stir it, don't worry or peek. Just leave it while you do yesterday's dishes. It will be light and fluffy with the grains all separate.

Mushrooms, green peppers, celery all sliced thin, small pieces of broccoli or leeks, almost any vegetable except potatoes are good as an addition to fried rice. Leftover pork, or beef, or chicken or turkey are all good in thin slivers, and canned lunchmeat or Chinese sausage – this is a cook's dish which just happens while you stand and talk.

The turmeric is a spice which you should be adventurous with. Keep turning the rice over as you add it. Don't stir, get your spoon or whatever underneath it, down at the bottom of the pan, and turn it over with a little care. And take it easy on the soy sauce until you have really tasted the turmeric.

Quicker to make than waiting for Chinese food to be delivered.

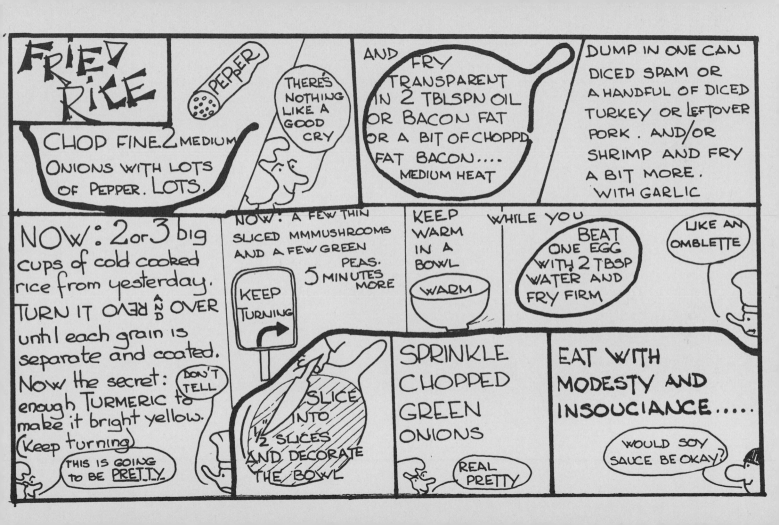

Saumon à l'Orange

19 This has to be one of the easiest and most pleasant ways to cook salmon. There's not even a cooking pan to wash.

Get salmon as thick as you can and as fresh as you can. And get a good dry vermouth. (I use Cazapras.) And remember that this fish is intended to be undercooked. Reduce the cooking time each time you do it, and see how much nicer undercooked fish is. And get the oven hot. Really hot.

Now, come home with the fish, put it to marinate in the vermouth (use enough – don't float it but let it soak in). That's all you do, just put it in a plate and forget it. And if you haven't yet discovered dry vermouth on the rocks now is the time. A glass, two ice cubes, two or three ounces of vermouth, and a slice of squeezed lemon peel. Sit down. Forget it. Dinner will be one hour and a bit. Talk to him, or her. Put your feet up, and if anybody asks you to do anything tell them you're busy – cooking dinner.

You can put the rice on half an hour before the fish is ready. Throw a few dried onion flakes in for a change, and a good knob of butter, or some fine chopped green onions, or some peas five minutes before it's cooked. Or put turmeric with it to make it pretty. This salmon needs something more than just rice. By this time you need some more vermouth in your glass, while you turn the salmon. Turn it a couple of times during the hour. That's not too hard, is it?

When you're ready, put each salmon steak on a sheet of foil. Sprinkle salt, quite a lot of dill and a big lump of butter. Now wrap it up. Get the edges all together and crimped and rolled over. Make it tight. And put it in the oven. If the oven is hot enough, no steak needs more than seven minutes. I have cooked whole fishes (five pounds) in less than twenty. Put it in, shut the oven door, and tip the vermouth from the marinade into a heavy saucepan. Grate, for each two people, the outer, coloured skin of an orange. Which, you may be delighted to know, is called the "zest." Make sure the orange peel is fine. If your grater is very coarse, then chop it a bit before using. Put it in the pan with the vermouth, and immediately the seven minutes is up pull out the packets of fish (use a glove), open one end of each, and pour the juices into the pan. Boil it on high heat for a minute or two. It will reduce quite noticeably. Meanwhile you are putting rice and things on plates, opening the packets of fish and looking smug.

Pour the sauce over the fish, and eat it.

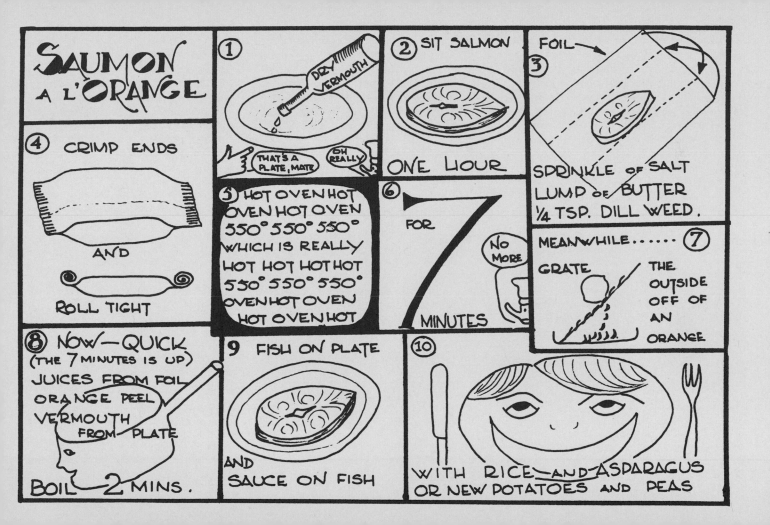

Sooper Stoo

Boeuf Catalan is an adaptation of a really magnificent Spanish stew. Preparation takes about fifteen minutes, after which you just leave it to cook. It is a weekend stew, something to make, put to cook, and forget about until you come home.

Just set the oven to its lowest setting, just under 200°F if you can, and certainly not above. The house will smell nice, and it is pleasant to come home after a movie, or skiing, or a walk in the rain.

For economy's sake, you can use dry cider instead of the wine and brandy, but the nutmeg and molasses are essential.

A pound and a half of stewing beef will feed four. Buy cheap bacon scraps – most of today's bacon is fat anyway, and all you want is the flavour.

Cooking at this low temperature also lets you cook overnight while you sleep. Then take it out of the oven, put in the refrigerator, and reheat whenever you need it.

Reheating is best done in a 350°F oven for twenty minutes or so – not on the top of the stove, where the bottom will burn unless you stir it, and stirring will turn it into mush.

This way, it is an attractive dish. Another advantage of low temperature cooking is that you can use any saucepan, even one with a plastic handle, because nothing burns. The meat won't shrink, and the wine won't evaporate – you get all you bought on your plate.

After you have made it the first time, you will be a stew cook, able to go anywhere in the world and be welcome. There are as many different stews as there are cooks, and don't let anybody tell you different. Be inventive. The only rule is not to boil or overheat.

If you like your stews thicker (this one is what the French call a knife-and-fork soup) pour off most of the gravy and thicken it by stirring in a couple of tablespoons of flour smooth in a little water. (Use a fork.) Boil it till it thickens, then pour it back on the stew.

Thick or thin, eat it with plain boiled potatoes and some nice people.

SOOPER STOO

BUILD IT LIKE THE PICTURE — TIGHT

TOMATOES
CARROTS
SLICED ONION
STEW BEEF
AND MUSHROOMS
SLICED ONION
CHEAP FAT BACON

AND
1 CLOVE GARLIC
½ TSPN NUTMEG
1 BAY LEAF
1 TSPN BOUQUET GARNI
OR
1 TSPN OREGANO

— HEAT ON TOP OF STOVE TILL BACON SMELLS GOOD —

ADD RED WINE TO HERE PLUS
1 OZ BRANDY
1 TBLSPN MOLASSES

BRING TO SIMMER PUT LID ON AND COOK 5 to 8 HOURS IN OVEN AT 200°

THAT'S A LONG TIME TO STAY IN THE BATH

CALL IT......
BOEUF CATALAN

YOU WILL BE AMAZED

Go Greek Cheap

21

Kids in the Middle East eat more tahini than North American kids eat peanut butter. It's a great sauce for chicken, with soda and a little garlic and maybe some lemon or a little grated ginger, and it's good for fish with white wine, but the nicest and simplest way of eating tahini is simply mixed with yogurt into a stiffish dip.

Tahini is ground sesame seeds. It is sold in most Greek stores and occasional Jewish delicatessens, in cans or in jars, and usually, by the time it gets off the shelf, the oil has separated and come to the top. So mix it with a fork.

Take about four good tablespoonfuls, chop a clove of garlic very fine, and mix it all together with the juice of a lemon. As you add the juice, it will get thick. Don't worry. Now add plain yogurt, a spoonful at a time, mixing it well, until you have a smooth, not too sloppy, dip-consistency bowlful.

Get a loaf of Greek bread, put the tahini in the best looking clay bowl you can find, and pull lumps off the bread. Pick up lots of tahini on the bread and eat it. It will stick to your teeth, which develops the need for retsina. So have a bottle open, and very cold, but don't put it in fancy, pretty little glasses. Drink it in big mouthfuls. After the first shock, you will love it or hate it. If you don't love it, you'd better go back to peanut butter.

Retsina is just about the worst wine in the world. The first mouthful tastes like paint remover. The second is something else. For some peculiar reason, it is almost hangover-free – which is worth remembering as it is so cheap and goes down so easily. The Greeks used to ship it in barrels of very new, very resinous cypress. At that time it was wine, still very bad wine, but recognizably wine when it started. But by the time it got to wherever it was going, the only taste left was the cypress resin. And people began to recognize it that way, and to like it. So that when it began to be shipped in bottles, they had to add resin to keep the flavour going.

Light the candle (I say candle because I buy altar candles from religious supply stores – you get a two-foot one of simple white wax for about $2.50 and it will burn for two or three days). And leave your guests to get on with things while you finish the rest.

Slice some tomatoes (the ripest you can find). Put them on a plate with olive oil, a good sprinkling of salt, and lots of fresh ground oregano. Lots. Then another layer and more of everything. Put it in the fridge for an hour or half an hour. Cut up feta cheese into half-inch cubes, open a can or two of anchovies, cut a green pepper into thin slivers, and cut some green onions into one-inch lengths.

When you are ready, take the tomatoes out of the refrigerator, decorate them with the anchovies, etc., and pour the oil from the anchovies over all. Forks if you must, but fingers are much better. I hope to get Colonel Sanders to try it, then he'll know what finger-lickin' good really means.

One thing more. Get olives, black ones, loose, not canned ones, oily and ripe, and put them with the tomatoes. You will probably need another loaf of bread.

go greek for $5

Open a bottle of Retsina and sip it

While you slice Tomatoes. Sprinkle with salt and ground oregano. Place in frig.

drink some more Retsina ½ hour later garnish with cubes of FETA

anchovies...
thin slivers of green pepper...
and green onions in 1" lengths

more Retsina while you make..

TAHINI
3 tbsp. Sesame paste. 1 clove chopped garlic juice of a lemon

These ingredients thicken as they are mixed. Add yogurt until dipping consistency

EAT WITH Greek bread fingers and more Retsina

preferably by candlelight

Fied Frish

22

Any fool can fry fish.

But frying is different. It is an old Japanese custom smuggled out of this country by a beautiful geisha girl who secretly fell in love with a drunken Irish sailor who, until he met her, ate nothing but chips and tomato ketchup. They settled down in one of the rare temperance districts of Ireland, where alcohol was purchased purely for medicinal purposes. The geisha girl, who could not abide tomato ketchup or french fries, agreed to modify the recipe to include beer, if her sailor would give up potatoes with his dinner.

The end result, fish with all kinds of vegetables, is delightful, a balanced meal which at one time gets the kids their vitamins and their father a case of beer. The improved diet so inspired the sailor that he became ambitious, emigrated to Canada, and exchanged the recipe for a left-handed screwdriver in order to go into business for himself.

The Japanese call this way of cooking Tempura. They cook prawns, and all kinds of fishes, and asparagus and green beans, and thin slices of sweet potato, and carrot sticks, mushrooms, cauliflower, broccoli, and best of all, celery tops.

The batter is extremely thin, without any of the soggy goo that packages most of the commercial fish. It almost looks as though there is not enough batter on the fish, but don't worry, let it drip off, fry it quickly (somewhere between 350 and 400°F) or with the oil hot enough to brown a half-inch cube of bread in half a minute.

I use sunflower seed oil, which is cheap and hardly smells at all. Ling cod is cheap, whole smelts are nice cooked this way, and everything is very pleasant eaten at once, sprinkled with a little lemon and garnished with fresh parsley.

You don't need any fancy equipment, just a saucepan, and the only important thing to remember is not to put too many pieces in at once, so that the oil doesn't cook too quickly.

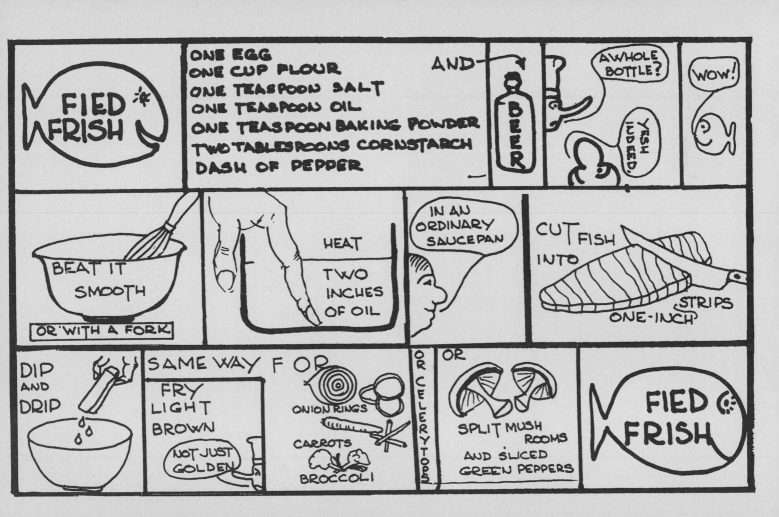

Slightly Pretentious Pork Chops

When you are in a hurry is no time to eat. This is a very simple, very easy and very satisfying dish that gives you at least half an hour to sit and reflect upon the injustices the world has this day wrought upon you. It is another frying pan dish, which needs a lid.

The ingredients are in most corner stores, so, even at midnight, if you want to cook, you can do it – if you have wine.

And, if you haven't, use apple juice. It will taste different. Not better, not worse (there are no absolutes in the vocabulary of a good cook), but just different.

Fresh pork is best, but even if the only chops you can get are frozen no matter – do just as the recipe says. But rub the paste well in with your fingers. Really rub it in. Don't lick your fingers – the sauce is pretty fierce until it is cooked.

If you like the pork and mustard flavour, you might like to try something really pretentious, which is almost as easy. It is called Pork Chops à l'Auberge du Grand Saint-Pierre and involves the same pork chops, trimmed the same, and then gently fried (medium heat) in oil and butter, after rubbing in a little pepper and salt.

Now make a paste of finely grated Gruyère cheese (about a quarter of a pound), two teaspoonfuls of mustard and enough whipping cream to make it all smooth. Spread it thickly on the chops, and put it under the broiler until the sauce is golden.

And, if you want to be Portuguese, or pretty close, sauté the outside of the chops, and dump a can of tomatoes and a bay leaf in the pan with them.

Let it all happen, then maybe some oregano and a little sherry, for about an hour. And, if you are going to be really Portuguese, leave all the fat on. Don't trim it at all.

The dish, with tomatoes, is almost infinitely expandable so that, if the smell leaks down the hall, and your friends stop by, just throw in some potatoes and another onion, and a bit more pepper and salt, and another bay leaf. If you haven't trimmed the pork, there will be flavour enough for ten.

SLIGHTLY PRETENTIOUS PORK CHOPS

 TWO EACH PORK CHOPS

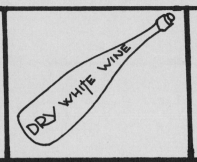 DRY WHITE WINE

 TRIM A BIT.

1/4 teaspoons PEPPER
1/2 MUSTARD
1 SALT
AND 4 TABLESPOON BUTTER

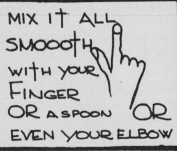 MIX IT ALL SMOOOTH WITH YOUR FINGER OR A SPOON OR EVEN YOUR ELBOW

 AND S-P-R-E-A-D IT ON THE CHOPS BACK AND FRONT

 CHOP AN ONION FINE

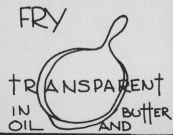 FRY TRANSPARENT IN OIL AND BUTTER

THEN THE PORK CHOPS - SAME PAN GOLDEN BROWN BOTH SIDES. ADD 1/4 OF THE WINE AND.....

45 minutes LID ON .....SIMMER.

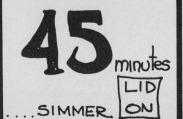 SPRINKLE WITH CHOPPED PARSLEY GOOD WITH NOODLES

The Best Fried Chicken in the World

24

One not too distant day it will appear on the television screens and the supermarket shelves, in the papers and the magazines, anywhere that a million dollars can buy advertising. And a million can-opening cooks will buy it and like all can-opening cooks, be disappointed without knowing why.

"SOUL" it will be called. "Just add a pinch to everything." There will be a picture of a smiling lady, and some smiling children, and perhaps a smiling man. Probably with Colonel Whatsit beaming from a background of smiling black faces. This recipe came to me from a smiling black face in the middle of New York. But she was careful to point out that soul isn't the monopoly of any colour or race and it doesn't come out of a bottle or packet. "It's sharing what there is with who there is." Princess Pamela has since written a cookbook, but long before that, when I was cold and had no money, she fed me fried chicken, gave me wine, and told me the recipe.

She had a little restaurant that seated sixteen. And she cooked in a kitchen the size of a broom closet, without fancy pots or thermostats – not even a fan. She measured things with the palm of her hand – a little palmful was a teaspoon, a big one a tablespoon. She fried in a big old pan with two or three inches of oil in it, and she always had the plates hot. And when she felt like it, she would sit down and talk to the customers.

You can cook this fried chicken on a two-burner hotplate with one saucepan – make the sauce first, then wipe it out and make the chicken. Strain the oil when it's cold through an old nylon stocking, and put it in a jar ready for the next time around.

If you want to cook for a lot of people, use a big roaster pan with two or three inches of oil in it, put the chicken in piece by piece so that the oil doesn't get too cool, and keep it warm in a low oven with the plates.

There's nothing else to say about the fried chicken except that it really is finger-licking good.

THE BEST FRIED CHICKEN IN THE WORLD

ONE EGG — BEAT LIGHTLY — ½ CUP MILK — IN ONE BOWL

MIX WELL — 1 CUP FLOUR - ½ TSPN SALT — ¼ CUP YELLOW CORNMEAL — ½ TSPN BAKING POWDER — DASH OF PEPPER — PAPRIKA — IN ANOTHER BOWL

WHAT ABOUT COLONEL JAUNDICE?

MAN, THIS CHICKEN GOT SOUL...

NOW

SAUCE BEEOOTIFUL

HALF CAN PEACHES
JUICE OF A LEMON
HALF CUP WATER
3 TBLSPN BROWN SUGAR
1 TBLSPN BUTTER
1 TBLSPN OIL
1 TBLSPN VINEGAR
HALF TEASPN PAPRIKA
SALT AND CAYENNE
TO TASTE

JUST HEAT TILL ITS THICK

DIP THE CHICKEN IN

EGG ETC — FLOUR ETC

AND FRY GOLDEN BROWN

DEEP HOT OIL

Hot Biscuits in a Hurry

Nothing looks more competent in a kitchen than baking. And there is nothing more rewarding for so little effort. A bit of flour, a bit of baking powder, a bowl, some fat and some milk, five minutes messing, fifteen minutes in the oven and there it is, hot and indigestible and a statement of love.

If you are going to graduate to bread, start with biscuits. You can be impressive at breakfast with them (or even more impressive in bed), very grandmotherly at teatime by the fire and extremely economical at suppertime with a poor man's soup and a basket full of hot biscuits. When you take them out of the oven put a cloth in the bottom of a bowl, then the biscuits, then wrap the ends of the cloth over to keep them warm.

And if it's two o'clock in the morning and you're hungry, try this instead of sending out for a pizza.

2 cups flour
1 teaspoon baking powder
1/2 teaspoon baking soda
1 teaspoon salt
3/4 cup milk
4 tablespoons shortening, or cooking oil (not olive) or butter.
1 cup sour cream

Mix all the dry things, pour in most of the milk, and make a stiff dough. Some flours take more milk than others. Knead it a little on a floured board (any flat surface dusted with flour will do), roll it out or pat it with your floury hand, anything to get it about a quarter-inch thick, cut it into rounds and bake fifteen minutes at 425°F.

If you want to be really clever, mix in a good handful of chopped or grated cheese and a sprinkle of cayenne just before you knead it.

If there are any left over, toast them for breakfast.

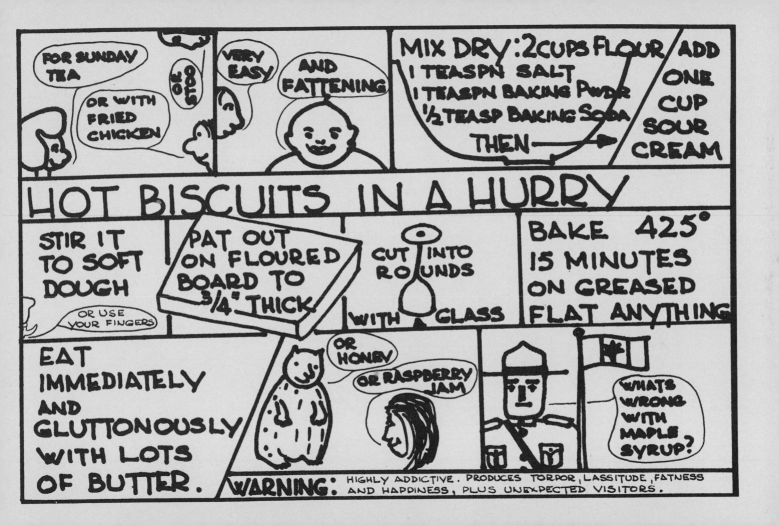

Quiche aux Fruits de Mer

26

Everybody should have one special party piece, something that's easy and not too complicated, and can be eaten hot or cold, and which is almost foolproof.

Quiche is just about all of these. It is luxurious, expensive, good hot, even better cold, and it can be used either as a special start to an otherwise simple meal (that way you get eight servings out of this recipe) or as a main course with consommé (four people) or as a really gluttonous late-night self-indulgence for two.

And it's flexible. Canned lobster is not quite as good as fresh, but crab can be used if you get some nice big chunks.

All you really have to learn is the simplicity of making pastry. Be quick, and be gentle, don't keep mauling it about with hot sticky hands. Then wrap it up. When it comes out of the fridge it may be just a little difficult to work, so let it sit for a while until it's easier.

The business of the beans or rice is called baking "blind." The beans are just to keep the bottom down and stop the sides falling in, and the fifteen minutes baking is to stop the bottom from getting soggy. If you feel really desperate to be proper cut a piece of foil to fit the bottom of the pastry and put the beans on that. But take it out before you make the final baking.

QUICHE aux FRUITS de MER

(speech bubbles: A SERIOUS AFFAIR · SOUNDS SOPHISTICATED · YEAH, BUT SO EASY)

① **PATE BRISEE.** (a very fancy name for pastry) • 8oz (1cup) plain flour
SIEVE (OR JUST FLUFF WITH A FORK) TOGETHER • level teaspn fine sugar
good pinch of salt

NOW: { QUICKLY GENTLY LIGHTLY }
(SORT OF TICKLE IT)

WITH YOUR FINGERTIPS RUB IN 5oz BUTTER. IN ¼" PIECES TILL IT LOOKS LIKE OATMEAL.
—
ADD ABOUT 2 TBLSP COLD WATER. ROLL INTO A BALL WRAP IN WAXED PAPER PUT IN FRIDGE ½ HR.

② **QUICHE Filling.**

BEAT A LITTLE FROTHY
¼ PINT WHIPPING CREAM
¼ PINT MILK · 4 EGGS
¼ PINT CLAM BROTH

③ **HALF an HOUR LATER**

ROLL OUT DOUGH ON FLOURED BOARD, ENOUGH TO LINE A 9" PIE TIN.

PRICK BOTTOM ALL OVER WITH A FORK. FILL WITH DRY BEANS OR RICE. BAKE 15 MINS. 450°

④ **OVEN TO 325°**

(speech bubble: TIP BEANS BACK INTO JAR)

ARRANGE ¼ SHRIMP AND AS MUCH LOBSTER AS YOU CAN AFFORD ON PASTRY. POUR QUICHE MIXTURE IN.

BAKE 40 MINUTES 325°

10,486·357 CALORIES

Lamb and Anchovies

This sounds completely ridiculous. I know. But just try it. Don't worry if you don't like anchovies, by the time they are cooked they taste totally different. And don't fall back on the usual "I hate lamb." This method will resurrect just about any old piece of mutton, but if you are careful and get a really nice piece of fresh local lamb from the butcher it is a delight whoever you happen to have for dinner. About three and a half pounds is the best size for four people. It will all get eaten hot, and the flavour is completely delightful

If you want to throw half a dozen medium-sized, peeled, whole onions into the pan an hour before it's cooked, that's nice. Then pour off the fat and make a little gravy. That's nice too. But nicest of all in lamb time is the zucchini time.

How to cook zucchini? Try this. Get nice, firm, good green zucchini. Slice them, unpeeled, into half-inch slices. Put a tablespoonful olive oil in your heaviest lidded saucepan, heat it medium till it's just short of smoking, and dump in the slices of zucchini with a clove of chopped garlic. Slosh them about a bit for three or four minutes until they start to cook, and while that is happening squeeze the juice of half a lemon (or more next time) over everything. Turn the heat down to simmer, put the lid on and leave it all for five minutes. Oh yes, and a little salt, and some people like a little pepper. Serve it in a dish with all the juices.

And, if you want a quick dessert, just sprinkle a little instant coffee, a little cocoa powder on vanilla ice cream, and pour ordinary whiskey over it. Carefully. This cuts the working time for a complete dinner down to something like twenty minutes.

LAMB AND ANCHOVIES

RIDICULOUS

I HATE LAMB

OKAY WAIT AND SEE

GET A FAT LAMB ROAST, BONE IN.

I LIKE LOINS

LARGE CLOVE CHOPPED GARLIC AND SMALL CAN ANCHOVY FILLETS, OIL AND ALL.

SMOOOTH IT— WOODEN SPOON

ADD TWO TBLSPN BROWN SUGAR. MAKE SMOOTHER

CRISS-CROSS FAT

SHARP KNIFE.

SPREAD ANCHOVY GUCK. PUSH IT INTO THE CRISSCROSSES AND ALL OVER.

HEAT 3 TBLSPN FAT IN 400° OVEN TO SIZZZLING. QUICK THE ROAST IN. BASTE AFTER 5, 10 AND 20 MINUTES.

OVEN TO 350° COOK A BIT LESS THAN 30 MIN/LB

ITS THE ONLY WAY TO GO

ESPECIALLY WITH ZUCCHINI.

Shepherd's Pie

28

This is a real idiot's recipe for the completely non-cook who wants to make a start somewhere. It is impossible not to make this well, and everybody loves it – the young, the toothless and the in-betweens, the cat and the girl in the next apartment. Everybody except the dog, because there never seems to be enough left for him. It's a social dish, two plates and two forks, and it's real cooking, home cooking.

In England, it is a Wednesday dish. Hot roast on Sunday, cold on Monday (washing day), curried roast on Tuesday and what's left over, ground up, in Shepherd's Pie on Wednesday. But it is much better made with fresh ground meat. It makes its own gravy, the top is crisp and brown and, if you are in a hurry or it isn't early summer when the fresh ones come, frozen peas are just great.

Try the peas this way. Two tablespoons butter in a saucepan, two tablespoons water. Half a teaspoon sugar, and a sprinkling of mint (fresh if it's available). Half a teaspoon salt. Heat, toss it about for three or four minutes.

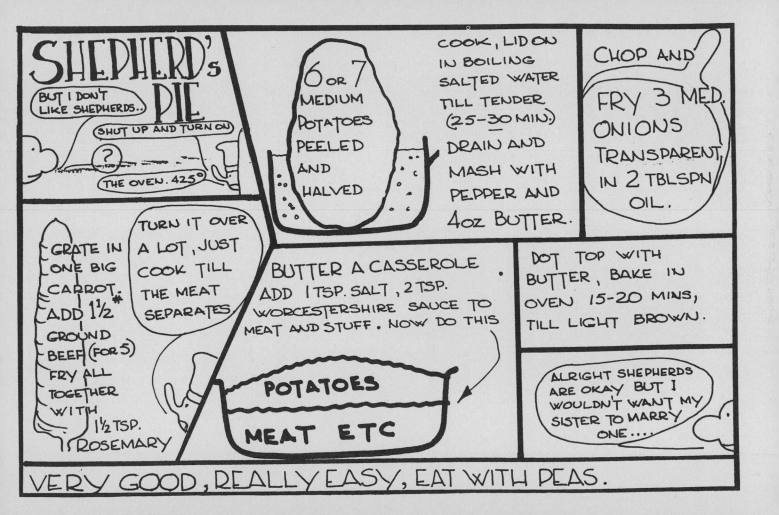

Almost Bisque

29 Let's be modest about this. Let's just say that it's the most luxurious, fattening, smooth, interesting, subtly-sophisticated soup anybody can make in half an hour, armed only with a can opener.

I discovered it late one night when a friend arrived unhappy. We made it while we talked.

Keep the heat down while you fry the onions, and keep it down while you simmer it all. The cloves, after twenty minutes, are just letting go their oil, which makes the flavour. Don't put too much sherry in, and don't let the onion get in any way crisp. This is a smooth soup.

If you can plan ahead, and get fresh crab, and cream, and some French bread, and a bottle of dry white wine, and a candle, and a bunch of daffodils, then you have a most elegant lunch in the pot. Otherwise, this is an incredible simple thing for late nights, for friends getting over the flu, for the day the mailman didn't come, or the end of a love affair. Smooth.

ALMOST BISQUE

①
CHOP A MEDIUM ONION FINE

VERY FINE

②
FRY IT GENTLY LIGHT BROWN

VERY LIGHT

IN 2 TBLSPN BUTTER

③
ADD

10 OZ. CAN TOMATO SOUP

10 OZ CAN WATER

1 BAY LEAF.

8 WHOLE CLOVES

JUICE ¼ LEMON

1 TSP. DILL

1 TSP. SUGAR

DASH OF PEPPER

2 PINCHES SALT

SIMMMER 10 MINUTES, LID ON.

ADD 2 OZ. DRY SHERRY OR 1 OZ BRANDY. SIMMMER 10 MIN. MORE. LID ON.

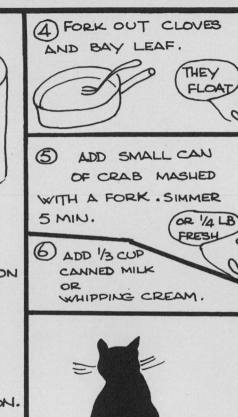

④
FORK OUT CLOVES AND BAY LEAF.

THEY FLOAT

⑤
ADD SMALL CAN OF CRAB MASHED WITH A FORK. SIMMER 5 MIN.

OR ¼ LB FRESH

⑥
ADD ⅓ CUP CANNED MILK OR WHIPPING CREAM.

Ginger Tea

30

This needs friends, and a candle too is nice, and a good dinner first is great and wine is always wine.

For each person: a mug full of water, an inch or so of fresh green ginger grated coarse into the saucepan, two heaped teaspoons brown sugar (or a bit more honey), and half a lemon (peel and all). Boil (lid on) ten to fifteen minutes.

Pour (strained – just hold back the shreds with something) into mugs and drink as hot as you can. The first sip liberates your taste buds (the Japanese do the same thing with sliced ginger for sushi), the second (which should be a good mouthful) clears your head, and half way through the cup you should get off – nice and warm and loose.

Avgolimono

31

Avgolimono is one of the smoothest, most delightful, and most surprising little soups I know. It is a little soup, not a great knife and fork effort or a cream soup with extra pans to wash, but just a simple little soup that tastes great, is elegant enough for anybody's dinner table, and gentle enough to be much appreciated during or after the flu.

Once you know how to make it you'll be able to do it with your eyes closed.

1. Hot chicken soup. I make my own, but cubes will work almost as well.

2. One egg for two people. Beat it well, until it's frothy and light.

3. Half a lemon per egg. Squeeze the juice very slowly; drop by drop into the egg. Keep beating for thirty seconds. Take it off the stove and serve.

It's a lovely colour, very good on a fall day.

Now, the serious business of chicken stock. I buy chicken feet in Chinatown on Saturday mornings. Or I buy chicken necks and backs at the butcher shop. All of which are very cheap. Take them home, dump them in a big pot, and cover with water. A veal knuckle is nice too, but it isn't essential. Put in a couple of onions, and carrots, and a stick or two of celery. A bay leaf and just a pinch of salt. You can add more salt when things are done, but just a little right now does things for the vegetable flavours. Bring it to a boil, and turn heat down to simmer. Five minutes later skim it with a spoon. If you get all the foam off the top the final stock will be clear.

Put the lid on tight, and simmer for a long time. I let mine do it all night and get up in the morning to memories of my grandmother. Strain it, and put it in jars, and use it for lots of things. Throw away the vegetables, and if you want a nice messy job take the meat off the chicken necks with your fingers.

Some fresh vegetables, sliced fine, some of the stock, a little salt and pepper and fifteen minutes cooking will make a good lunch with fresh bread.

The stock will jell in the fridge. Use it as you would soup cubes, for Chinese food, stews, for cooking cabbage and peas, for making spaghetti sauce, or borscht.

Eight-Hour Chicken

32

Forget all the brainwashing about high temperatures, about 450°F for an hour, then exactly 400°F for twenty minutes. And at the same time forget all about the expensive cuts of meat, except for very special occasions. Forget also about TV dinners, or hurried hamburgers. Just get up, put the chicken in the oven, and forget about it. If your oven will set at lower than 200°F, then set it there, somewhere around 175°F if you can, and then forget it for even longer.

You can, at the same time forget all about cleaning the oven, because with low temperature cooking there is no fat splashing around, just a gentle, warm comfortable happening.

Try it first with a cheap chicken. Come home, put some rice or potatoes on the fire. Put a few instant onions or chopped onions in with the rice if you like, and a little bit of butter, and five minutes before it is cooked a few frozen peas. Sprinkle a little curry powder on the rice, and there's dinner, the inside of the chicken filled with juice which also is nice on the rice, and the meat moist and tender. Some ovens turn the skin into a brittle, parchment-like affair, which you just discard; others get it brown and crispy.

Sometimes I cover the pan loosely (just lay it on) with foil and sometimes I just leave things as they are. The most successful meal I have ever cooked this way was one evening or early morning when I came home drunk, got into bed, and remembered I had guests coming for lunch. I crawled out of bed, pulled the chicken out of the fridge, and managed, at the third attempt, to get it into the frying pan. And the frying pan, at the fourth attempt, into the oven.

There it lay, until my guests woke me next day. They were very smug, but not half as smug as I was when twenty minutes after they arrived they were sitting down to roast chicken.

This is a technique that will teach you to cook. You make your own mind up about what you like best, make notes, and almost anything you do will be right. Eight hours, ten hours, it doesn't really matter.

Try it with cheap frozen lamb rubbed with oregano and garlic. Get a cheap roast of pork and treat it to lots of basil and a little pepper and salt. Get a cross rib roast; massage it with garlic and pepper and salt. Get an old duck, or a real monster of an old goose that has to be cheap, poke an onion or two inside and maybe an orange. Forget it. Don't worry. Write a book. Teach yourself to crochet. Join Men's Lib.

But forget the dinner until you are ready.

Smelt Teriyaki

33

On all the shores of North America, in the summer and at midnight, there are men and boys catching, one way or another, smelt. Sometimes they dip nets on poles, sometimes they hang nets in the water at the turn of the tide, and sometimes they wade in with lanterns. They all have different tricks, and they all catch fish, and they all take them home in a bucket to cook.

All except those who take them to the fishmonger, who sells them, usually cheap. You can fry them dipped in flour, or make them very pompous dipped in egg and breadcrumbs, or you can try this recipe, which is so delicious that you will never try any of the others.

Don't clean them; just wipe them, lay them in the pan, head on and all, and cook them whole. Turn them carefully – they will be a burnished coppery colour where they have been fried – and eat them like you play a mouth organ, using your front teeth the way they were designed for, nibbling the flesh off the bone like a mouthful of midnight ear. Very nice.

Fry anything in the same mixture of oil and soya sauce and sugar. The Japanese call it Teri-Yaki.

And of course, you take the stuff out of the fridge and eat it. Its called Sunomono.

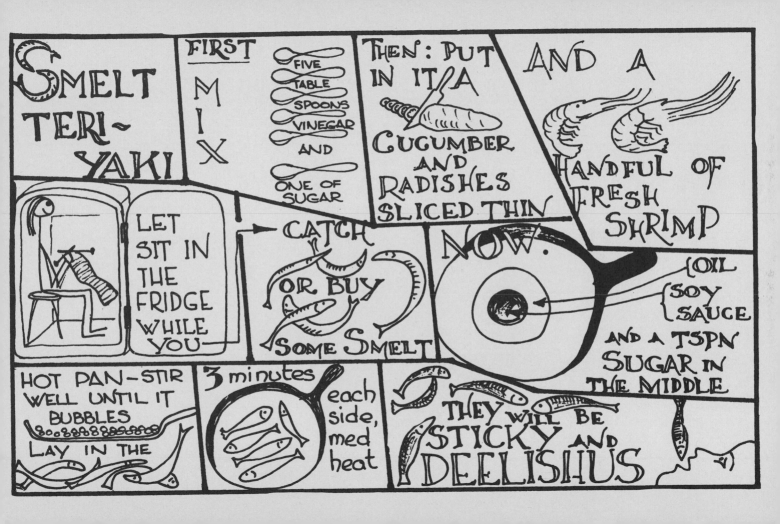

Chinese Beef

34

Any fool can cook a steak. All you need is enough money to buy it and a really hot fire.

But cooking meat the Chinese way costs a lot less, takes no more time, and leaves enough money left over for a bottle of wine.

This is a quick and simple trick given me with love by an old friend and dedicated cook, Alex Louie of Vancouver's Marco Polo restaurant. He sells a lot of it; my friends eat a lot of it.

One flank steak will feed four people, with vegetables and rice. If there are only two of you, take a knife, cut the steak in half, and keep the rest for tomorrow.

The secret in all Chinese fry cooking is in getting the pan much hotter than you think it should be. Really hot. I heat it up, with no oil in it, till drops of water flicked on it bounce. Then (very quick) the oil, the garlic, the ginger and piece by piece the beef, turning everything constantly.

And if you want a change for the next day, buy some star anise, crunch it up and add that instead of the ginger.

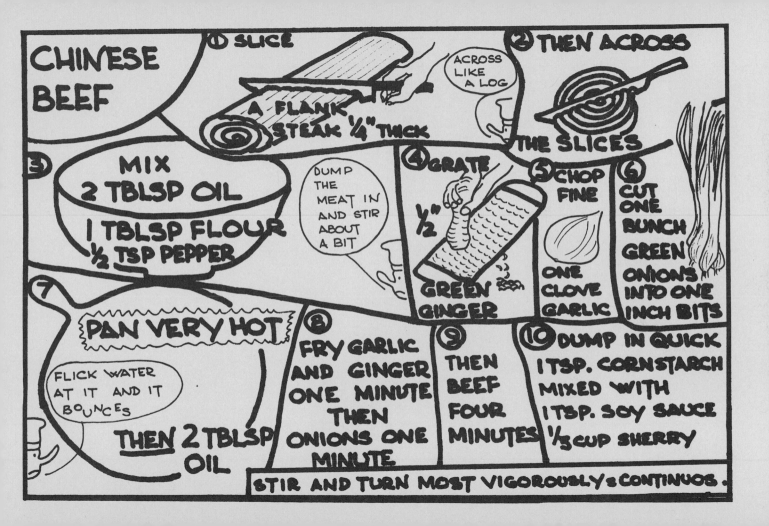

Just Enough Jam

35

My grandmother lived in the same house for fifty-seven years. It was the jam that kept her there. She was good at it, and also miserly. The cupboards of her kitchen, the tops of her closets, the basement, even suitcases under the bed, were full of jam. Strawberry jam, blackberry jam and even turnip jam. If we were very good we were allowed to eat it, on fresh bread, which she was also very good at.

Nobody wants an apartment full of jam today, but it is nice, each time a new summer fruit appears fresh in the stores, to make it just once, just enough for a couple of breakfasts or tea with some friends. Or pancakes.

This way of making jam is foolproof, and it tastes nice, without any of the pectin or other mystiques that usually seem to go into jam making.

If you buy strawberries by the pound, then the proportions are correct. If you buy a twelve-ounce packet, which for some reason appears to be popular with the supermarkets, then use two-and-a-quarter cups of sugar and most of the juice of the lemon. You can put the rest in gin.

And if you want to be super conservative, peel the lemon first in a long thin spiral, just the yellow part. Then poke it into a mickey of gin, and leave it for a week or two. Nice, clean-tasting lemon gin – very good for summer.

Most other summer fruits will also make jam. Just use three-quarters of the sugar you do for the strawberries.

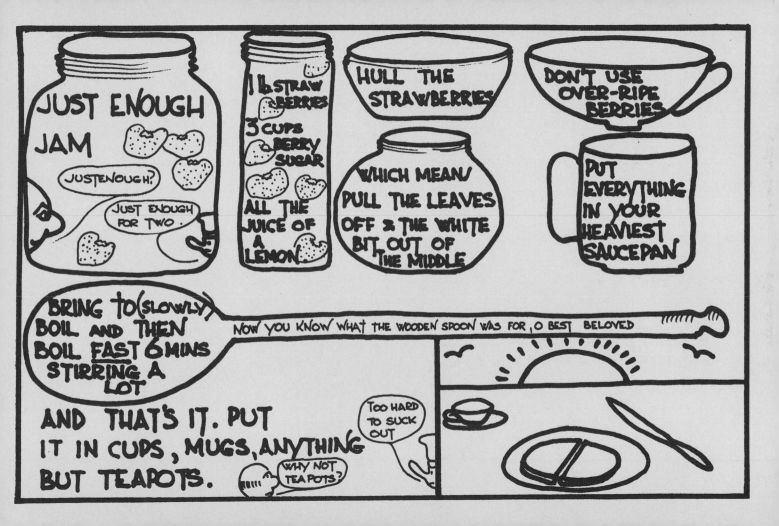

Turkey Tremenjus

36

There is just no way to describe this turkey, other than the friendliest cooking you will ever experience. I mean, you need friends for a turkey, just to eat it, so you might as well get them there early and spend the day doing it.

We sit around and smoke a bit, and drink a little, and tell lies. Somebody gets up to look at it, or baste it, or just smell it, every fifteen minutes or so, and people go for walks and get hungry, or play with whatever the kids got for Christmas.

It looks really terrible. The first time I tried it I was most ashamed - everybody's dinner was ruined and I was going to write letters to the newspaper I got it from, and Pierre Berton and Himie Koshevoy – and all the other people who had recommended it – but we all kept basting and sipping and finally we fished it out and did what the book says. It was magnificent, like a twenty-pound pheasant. Get one between eighteen and twenty-two pounds, and a dozen or so friends. Happy Christmas, or Thanksgiving, or whenever you decide to do it.

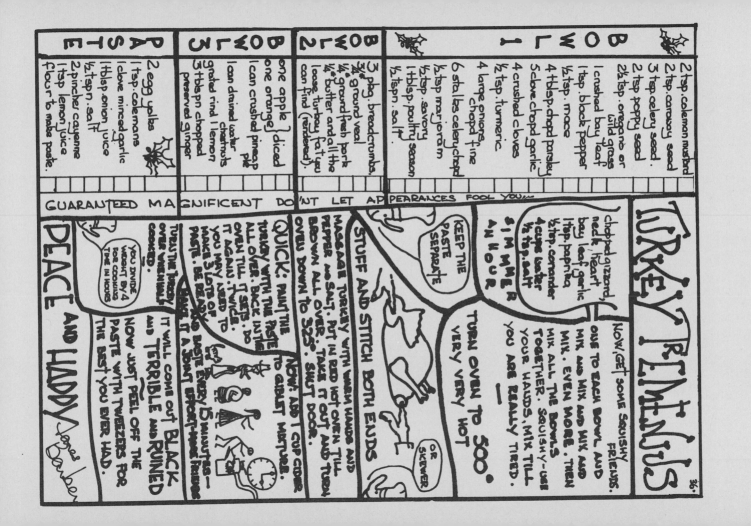

Christmas Drinks

37

Hot tea is the simplest of all hot drinks. My grandmother loved it. With half an inch of whiskey in the bottom of the cup. I still do it, on Sunday afternoons, when it's raining. And the same amount of brandy in a cup of coffee has considerable merit.

But it seems that Christmastime is the time for getting sentimental about hot toddies, and punches, and Wassail Bowls, so most people get out a tin saucepan and a bottle of the cheapest, and boil it with cinnamon or detergent of whatever takes their fancy, and drink it quick and spend the next two days bragging about their hangover.

Next time you make a hot drink, try using your best booze, and your best saucepan, and don't boil it, just make it hot enough in small quantities, and find your way into a pleasant warm nodding happiness.

When you make the Yard of Flannel, try using two jugs, one for the hot ale, the other for the eggs and things. Pour them one into the other, back and forth, till they are smooth.

And if you want a very pleasant occupation, try Charles Baker's English Bishop. First you take an orange and stud it all over with whole cloves. Dip it in brandy and roll it in brown sugar. Put it on a stick and toast it over the fire till the sugar caramelizes. Now cut it into quarters, put it in a pan with a bottle of the best port you can find, and just simmer very gently for twenty minutes with the lid on. Add four ounces of brandy, and warm another ounce in a spoon. Just before you serve it, pour the brandy (the spoon-warm brandy) gently on to the saucepan and set fire to it. Very potent. But you must not boil it; boiling ruins any wine for drinking and port most of all.

Happy Christmas!

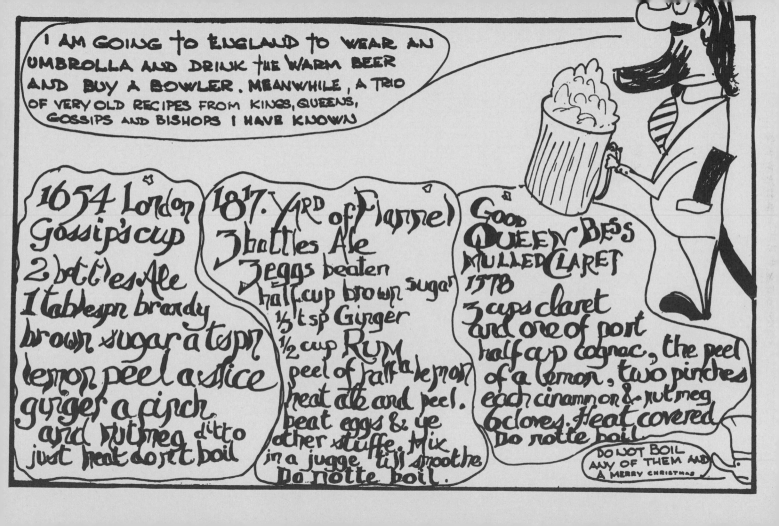

Pork Chops Canadiennes à la Façon de Kelowna

38

It smells so nice. Like an old French kitchen with a pot on the stove. I learned to cook with apple juice in Normandy where the apple is a large and important part of the farm economy. They make cider from it, and a most lethal drink called Calvados. The girls use it for their complexions (and there is nothing like an armful of girl smelling of fresh pressed apples), the pigs eat a lot of them, and in fall the pork takes on a very interesting colour and flavour.

There are not many apple-fed pigs in North America, but if you want to get the special flavour, here it is, sort of sweet, a little spicy from the cinnamon and very tender. I eat it with heavy rye bread and asparagus when it's in season.

Bon appétit.

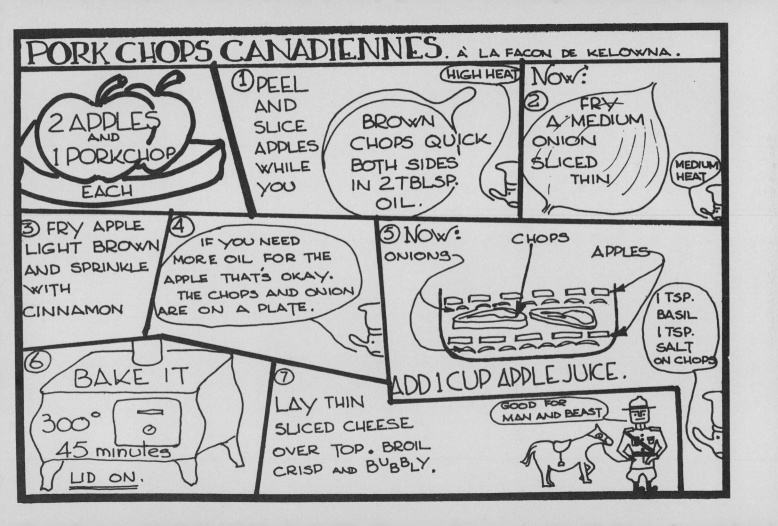

Cauliflower Cheese

39 Next time you have vegetarians to dinner, or cauliflowers are cheap, or you have a very simple boiled chicken, try your hand at this.

Just be careful making the sauce. Cook it slowly at first, then add the stock (cubes or real) slowly, and the milk slowly, keeping the temperature up while you do it so that you can see how thick or thin it is getting.

Warm the egg yolks with some of the sauce before you mix them all together (this will stop the yolks curdling), and that's about all you have to worry about. If you want to be really luxurious, use heavy cream instead of the milk, and omit the egg yolks altogether. And if you want to be downright extravagant, use white wine instead of stock.

And if you want to be different, give it a good dusting of nutmeg before you pour the sauce over the cauliflower.

This very simple dish has a habit of becoming a household standby.

Ice Cream and Whisky

40 Oh those pillow-warm and plumply pretty

Girls who live in every city

Never whistled at by any

Men who think it highly bene-

ficial to their status

to take out girls not quite so fat as

the placid, kind and all-forgiving

chubbies who think cheesecakes's living.

Turkey Tarragon for Two

41 This is a very simple version of a well-known classic. *Poulet a l'Estragon*. It was taught to me by a girl in Normandy, who also taught me to steal chickens.

The chickens of Normandy were big and tough and old. And the stolen ones were cheap. Turkey legs are a substitute that fills most of these requirements, but if you do happen to have a butcher who keeps his chickens Normandy-farmer-style he will probably expect you to steal them.

So here's how you do it. The chickens sleep in apple trees, on branches about four feet off the ground. They must be snuck up upon, very quietly, from behind, with one hand from above, and one from below. You very carefully and slowly bring the two hands together at exactly the same moment, keeping firm hold with the lower one while the upper one helps the chicken off the branch quietly and quickly under your jacket. You then run.

My instructor was a purist. She felt that chicken stealing was a natural predatory act, in tune with nature. In order to get properly in tune, etc., she insisted that we spend the evening waiting for the right moment (usually two or three in the morning) getting our natural rhythms ready.

So if you have a butcher whose chickens sleep in trees in an apple orchard which has a haystack close by, all you need is a partner interested in natural rhythms and you will have a really authentic Normandy chicken.

If you haven't got arrowroot, use two teaspoons cornstarch. But arrowroot is much better; it's smoother, and translucent.

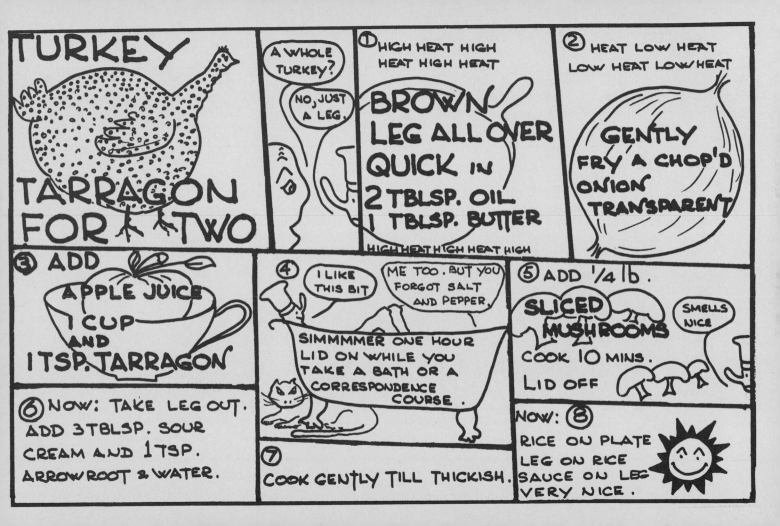

Salade d'Haricots Verts au Gruyère

42

Contrary to popular opinion, what French girls really do is make salads. A simple roast chicken, a salad, some fresh bread and a bottle of wine make a memorable meal without most of the panic that accompanies North American dinners.

This salad, which, in spring and summer, when the beans are fresh and young, is very close to being one of the greatest salads in the world, is simple, classic and typically French. It comes (for snob interest) from La Comtesse Guy de Toulouse-Lautrec. On its own it is a very pleasant lunch. With a few trimmings it transforms the simplest dinner.

You can, if you must, use frozen beans. But try it with the fresh ones, the skinniest you can find, the greenest you can find, and the flavour is sophisticated enough for adults, simple enough for children. Make enough. Make lots. It is not a salad to be sneaked on to the corner of a plate and nibbled at.

The secret is in making the vinaigrette – which is simply a French dressing with stuff in it. Once you have made it, it will keep for a long time anywhere reasonably cool. But if you refrigerate it too much, the oil turns into a lump at the top of the bottle, which requires warming under the hot tap, then shaking.

Put whatever you fancy that is fresh in it. If you use bottled herbs, like tarragon, crush them first between two spoons to liberate the flavour. Shake it a lot. This is another standby which easily becomes a family favourite.

Velvet Chicken and Mushrooms

43

Fresh ginger you can buy in almost any enlightened supermarket, strange lumpy-looking tan-coloured roots, from Hawaii. And they are something you should learn to use.

Most simple Chinese vegetable dishes are flavoured with fresh gingerroot, just a bit, shredded into bean sprouts. And most very bad Chinese restaurant food is made with shredded cooked chicken. If you learn to use fresh chicken, cut to size before it is cooked, and cooked very little, you will quickly come to an appreciation of what Chinese food really tastes like.

It's quite easy. All you need is a sharp knife. Slide it close to the bones, and get off as much meat as you can in one piece. What is left on the bones will, with an onion, and simmered gently while you eat dinner, make a magnificent light soup for tomorrow's dinner, particularly if you remember to bring home a few mushrooms to slice into it, and even more particularly if you shred just a little ginger into it while it simmers.

This particular recipe is called Maw Gwooh Chow Ghuy Pien if you want to be smart. It is very simple, very smooth, and very spicy, a quick and easy thing to make in fifteen minutes. Just don't overcook it. Don't overcook it. Don't overcook it.

The chicken will turn a nice delicate white. If you want to make it even more exotic (although this is, I think, an unnecessary sophistication), replace a glass of the stock with a glass of sherry. But whatever you do, don't overcook it.

Aunt Pamela's Sunday Pork Roast

44

Aunt Pamela is not really very nice at all. She is a garrulous old windbag who has talked three husbands to death. But she can cook. That's how she catches them. She does this on Sundays in spring, when pork is cheap. She spends the afternoon looking smug; nipping in and out of the kitchen in her apron, and suddenly everything is ready, all on one dish. She talks and everybody else eats. It's very good. A five pound roast will feed about twelve people. Or four teenagers.

If you get organized first, peel the potatoes and quarter them, peel the onions and cut the carrots so they are all about as thick as your thumb. There's nothing to do for the rest of the afternoon except smell it cooking. After the first twenty minutes it is a nice cinnamon colour, and it gets darker and darker until it's ready. You can use zucchini instead of carrots, or leeks, or celery. But keep the onions, they're nice.

And if you have any spare room in the oven, put a couple of apples apiece in a baking dish. Don't peel them, just cut out the cores and fill them with brown sugar and raisins. Push it in tight with your thumb, and heap it tight on top. Put a little water in the pan and bake them for an hour, basting occasionally. Very good with ice cream. And a little cinnamon in the sugar is good. Pour the juice over it all.

And the meat gravy. No flour, just a little stock, scrape well around the bottom of the pan and mix it well while it boils down. Happy Sunday.

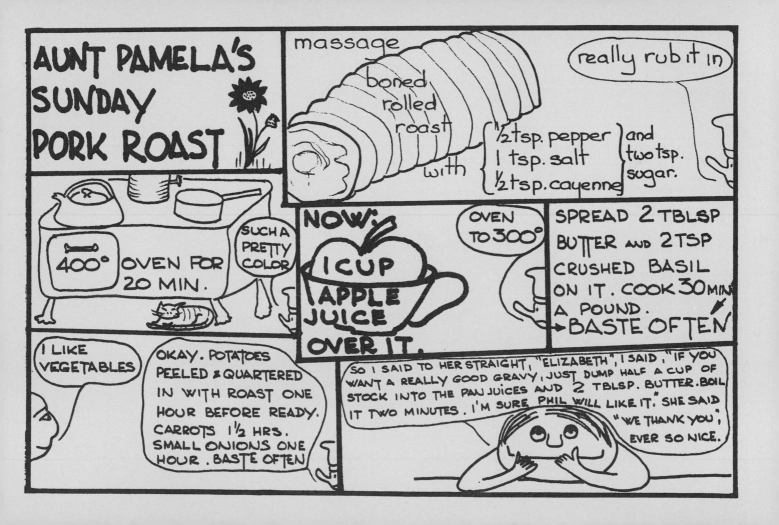

Pescado del Carmen

45

I can never understand why the recipes for swingers go in for beef tenderloin.

"Hello?"

"Susan?"

"Yes, John?"

"I've got Pescado del Carmen."

"You've got what?"

"Pescado del Carmen."

"Is that a new car?"

"No, it's something I picked up in Mexico."

"Oh no. Who did you get it from?"

"A fisherman's wife in Baja California."

"Are you sure?"

"Of course I'm sure."

"Well what shall I do?"

"Come round if you like. Ever had it?"

"Certainly not. You are awful. What shall I tell people?"

"You don't have to tell anybody anything. Just come round. It smells very interesting."

"John, you're disgusting."

"Look, what's disgusting about a fantastic, cheap, really ethnic dinner full of nourishing vitamins and exciting tastes? Pescado del Carmen is much better than all that phony Mexican stuff made of beans."

"Oh."

"Well, are you coming?"

"Yes… John?"

"Yes?"

"I'm so glad you've got Pescado del what-sit."

"What do you mean?"

"Look, I'll be round later."

Index